THROUGH THE LENS OF THE WORLD HEALTH CRISIS PART 1

Ethical Dilemmas

Sofia Laurden Davis

iUniverse LLC
Bloomington

THROUGH THE LENS OF THE
WORLD HEALTH CRISIS PART 1
ETHICAL DILEMMAS

iUniverse books may be ordered through booksellers or by contacting:

iUniverse LLC
1663 Liberty Drive
Bloomington, IN 47403
www.iuniverse.com
1-800-Authors (1-800-288-4677)

ISBN: 978-1-4917-3534-3 (sc)
ISBN: 978-1-4917-3535-0 (e)

Library of Congress Control Number: 2014909122

Printed in the United States of America.

iUniverse rev. date: 05/20/2014

To everyone who is partially and fully involved in business, community, pharmaceutical, biotechnology, and research organizations, as well as nurses, individuals, and others in health care industries, including all medical doctors past, present, and future.

To my grandson, Rael; to my sons, Rhoss and Danny, and their wives, Tara and Brenna; and to my husband, Tom Davis, my confidante.

CONTENTS

Introduction

My husband, Tom, loves to watch western movies wherein a doctor travels to a patient's house to treat the sick; in the old days, this practice was quite common. Medical doctors prioritize their patients and listen to them sensibly with passion and willingness to help and aid them. My younger son, Danny, will become a medical doctor in the near future, and I would like my son to prioritize his patients. Passion is the key to people who need us so we may influence others' lives.

However, this practice no longer exists. We are now living in a pluralistic society. I fear that a pluralistic society influences our children and that good decision making is off the table. I arrived at the conclusion that we may have to start offering ethics classes in charter and public schools to influence our young minds of our good, God-given wisdom. With our own eyes, we have witnessed the struggles of humanity, the struggles of addiction to the pill mill.

I have witnessed, with my own eyes, patients' experiences in their doctors' offices. Patients must wait and are called by numbers or by last names, supposedly. Every time a patient visits his or her doctor for a little advice, the patient must pay. Whether a patient pays a co-pay or the whole bill, little aches and pains have led us to a McDonald's-ized health care industry. Then some used their creativity and developed the walk-in clinic. Humans learned that a doctor must examine every ache and pain. The society relied on medical technology— most individuals thought that drugs were the trick to living long lives. Somehow, the society was numbed and blinded, unable to distinguish between good medicine and bad medicine.

My analysis is that this is just one of many reasons individuals end up misusing drugs that come with easy access and availability.

Besides my continuing education, I am also a current and active volunteer advocate for neglected and abused children. Most of my cases involve parents who are in jail due to drug abuse and domestic violence charges. One of my cases involved a prekindergarten, five-year-old boy. At the time I was assigned this case, the boy was taking seven types of medications as an ADHD patient. I found that this child did not need those medications. With my comments, reports, and input from the boy's schoolteachers, I managed to remove four of the seven medications. With help from doctors, agencies, and health care professionals, this boy is currently with a licensed foster parent and living a normal life. Each case has its own story waiting to be told. The problem was where to begin to tell the stories. So I thought to use the lens of the ethical dilemmas humans and organizations have encountered (and are likely to encounter in the future).

At the time writing this book, I was in the process of attending the commencement ceremony for my PhD in human services, specializing in management of nonprofit agencies and leadership. It was a long journey. I have written many theses from previous class assignments and have been able to keep all of my writings, one of which was about the ethical dilemmas every individual and organization must go through. Publication of my dissertation is a ticket to qualify me to be called a doctor of philosophy (PhD). Therefore, my motivation to write the philosophical view of an ethical dilemma was just the beginning of my traverse through the world of common sense, something we should all possess.

For some reason ethics are very difficult to define. Balancing right and wrong decisions may be the best solution; however, individuals get caught up in making the right decision, ending up with the wrong one instead. Due to vast responsibilities on both sides of the organizations involved, how does an individual or an organization grasp what is logical or comprehensive to follow rules and regulations for the sake of social responsibility? Continuing to see what happened when it came to ethically responsible individuals, we may also blame our acculturated humanity and what we have learned from our ancestors and the community we live in. Where should an organization or an individual's creativity stand when profit comes before social responsibility?

Should a corporate leader or the person who is responsible choose social responsibility before corporate profit? Does the organization or the individual think that the answer from critics of neoclassical economics would be no? Neoclassical economics prioritize corporate profit over social responsibility for sustainability (Davis 1998). It may be the right decision because corporation have to profit in order for the business to continue its service. To prevent any mishaps, organizations would then write and develop their own policies, procedures, and codes of ethics. Does a code of ethics really work?

Chapter 1
POLICIES, PROCEDURES, AND A CODE OF ETHICS

Matching a nonprofit organization's values with the values of stakeholders, customers, and vendors is important for balancing interests of different group members and cultures. "Nonprofit Organizations must realize the importance of extending their ethical mission beyond their immediate circle so that their values are matched by vendors, organization members, customers, and other stakeholders" (Gray, 121). These policies and action should be developed and agreed upon by members of the organizations to incorporate the values of stakeholders. Code alone is not the solution to the problem; however, many organizations these days are embracing the code of ethics. Gray said that through honesty and good, right conduct, business leaders should possess good leadership skills and should lead by example (Gray 122).

1

Meanwhile, all companies and organizations have ethical obligations to their employees, such as the following: a right to privacy, a right to not be fired without cause, a safe workplace, due process, fair treatment, freedom of speech (whistle-blowing), and an environment that is free of bias (Trevino and Nelson 2007, 233). Trevino and Nelson continue on to write, "Organizations also have a clear ethical obligation to shareholders and other owners" (p.233) such as serving the interests of owners, and the future health of the organizations. We are all responsible in all of these ethical dilemmas. We are now living in a fast-paced, multitasking work environment, and it's too easy to forget the importance of good, ethical behavior in what we do at work and home that will affect our environment. According to Trevino and Nelson, "The ethical obligation implicit for all of us is to think long term about the health of the planet and its environs for ourselves, our children, and other generation to follow" (244).

In the text of Trevino and Nelson, there are eight steps company leaders should follow as ethical decision makers:

1. Gather the facts.
2. Define the ethical issues.
3. Identify the affected parties (the stakeholders).
4. Identify the consequences.

5. Identify the obligation.

6. Consider your character and integrity.

7. Think creatively about potential actions.

8. Check your gut. (103-109)

In Posavac and Carey's text, on page 96, ethical principles adopted by the American Evaluation Association are listed. This is believed to be the code of ethics or credo for guidance.

1. Systematic inquiry

2. Competence

3. Integrity/honesty

4. Respect for people

5. Responsibility for general public welfare

We may express daunting questions: How can an organization balance a code of ethics against sustaining the organization's ability to make a profit? Where do we draw the line between corporate responsibility and social responsibility? Giving examples of pharmaceutical and biotech and its pill mill industries, down to how pills are used by the society for aches and pains and how our children affected by these actions of our citizens can have a devastating effect for the rest of us.

Chapter 2
RIVER BLINDNESS

A Closer Look at Pharmaceutical
and Biotechnology Industries

Today, the world health crisis is an overwhelming issue. The deepest concerns and answers to most of our questions rely on the research facing ethical dilemmas by pharmaceutical and biotechnology industries. We are all affected by these ethical dilemmas, and we can conclude that partly the causes of world health crisis, created by companies such as pharmaceutical and biotechnology, affect us all. Through the vine, some would say that medical doctors and health care industries are not alone in the blame of the world's health crisis but also I say to each everyone of us who have witnessed and did not do any action to stop this devasting life routine is part to be blamed.

For the sake of an example in the case of river blindness, or onchocerciasis, the explanation begins with how pharmaceutical and biotechnology companies operate, which helps us understand why cost of the drug to treat the disease is so high, and why the trend of health crisis is an overwhelming issue. How do pharmaceutical and biotechnology companies balance corporate profits against social responsibilities?

There are ethical concerns about gaining corporate profits at the expense of social responsibilities. Perhaps the most controversial issues in the pharmaceutical industry are the current economical situation, an increase in global health problems, difficulty in sustaining social responsibilities, and unencumbered corporate profits. The ethical dilemma is whether to first consider corporate profits before social responsibilities. In addition, nonprofit organization funding mostly comes from stakeholders' investments, private and public donations, and government agency funding. "As with other fields, there is now an increased public consciousness and focus on the part of funding agencies on these ethical issues" (Aultman and Walker, 1). Some say, in today's economy, that venture capital funding is risky. However, philanthropist giving has skyrocketed since the publication of high-profile diseases surfacing in developing countries overseas. The funding is invested to conduct research on cures for diseases such as malaria, HIV/AIDS, and river blindness (onchocerciasis).

Recently, the success of Merck & Co., Inc. with Ivermectin (Mectizan) still has some issues to be resolved. There are long-term strategy requirements to secure gains and accomplishments made so far. Meanwhile, the World Bank's recent agenda is to reduce or to discontinue funding for river blindness. In addition, articles found, which will be explained later, state that there will be no incentives to continue to develop the drug research because the country is so poor and no one can afford the drug. When a company anticipates zero return on investment, it is impossible to continue a long-term commitment to the production of the drug. However, are corporate profits achieved by producing drugs for aches and pains? Isn't the society overrun by these drugs that are somehow misused?

There are challenges among underlying ethical issues in global health problems, such as sustaining social responsibilities, ethical statuses, moral statuses, and corporate profits that are complicated to define. Many questioned the ethical nature of Merck & Co., Inc. and World Bank discontinuing support for river blindness research. The stakeholders, government, and private supporters are hesitant to invest because of the current economy situation. We may ask how a company can sustain its responsibility if corporate profit is not achieved.

However, we don't believe that a reputable company would discontinue such research for a drug in a time when people are suffering! Therefore, we make our own judgments. Each one of us differs on how we proceed with our judgments, and we may think we made a judgment fairly enough to say that people who are suffering have to be considered first. For example, we may not be aware that the Amazon rainforest has a role in the ecosystems to stabilize regional and global climate (Davis 1998).

Meanwhile, the recent study is focused on river blindness, which has affected eighteen million people worldwide. The rest were cured through the drugs produced by Merck. This infectious onchocerciasis is a parasite carried by black flies, which feed on human blood, that cause itching, leave worms inside the human body, and create havoc physically and psychologically. An infected person may die if not treated. In 2005 alone in Africa, there were ninety million at risk were infected which estimated to 37 million people that carry onchocerciasis volvulus. There are 500,000 cases of severe visual impairment and 270,000 of blindness due to onchocerciasis. Therefore, to elaborate there is a possibility that onchocerciasis could spread globally—that includes the United States of America (Garret 2007; Mackie, Taylor, et al. 2006; Carbone 2000; Richard-Lenoble, et al. 2003).

Furthermore, Basanez, Pion, et al., explain that onchocerciasis spread to six Latin American countries from its origin in West Africa (2006, 1454). They concluded that in the Simulium damnosum sensu lato (s.l) species complex, which includes approximately 60 cytoforms, is responsible for more than 95 percent of onchocerciasis cases globally. In Latin America about 360,000 people are at risk, Colombia and Ecuador has 24,600 at risk, northern Venezuela has 104,500, and southern Venezuela and Brazil has 20,000. O. Volvulus is endemic in 27 sub-Saharan African countries, and was imported through the slave trade to six Latin American countries. Previous estimates have placed the number of people infected worldwide at 18 million, of which 99 percent were in Africa. Since then, the true extent of the disease has been estimated by the rapid epidemiological mapping of onchocerciasis (REMO).

In addition, Kenya, Rwanda, and Mozambique were found not to be endemic (a native land of or particular place where the disease settled). However, these countries were protected by Onchocerciasis Control Programme (OCP) umbrella (Basanez, Pion, et al., 1457). The social-responsibility/corporate-profit dilemma collide in many aspects of accountability. Pharmaceutical companies such as Merck, Co., Inc. and GlaxoSmithKline are partnered to combat the complexity of onchocerciasis ovulvus.

However, the CEO of Merck & Co., Inc. is planning to discontinue the research of the drug because the project is categorized as zero return on investment (Drisdelle 2003).

The article by Garret (2007) explores the possibility of private and public donations given for global health problems. However, the funds received by the companies are spent on specific, high-profile diseases rather than for public health in general. We may wonder what type of research of specific, high-profile diseases are the donations meant to fund? Garret continues to say that there is a danger for this uncoordinated distribution of funding. In addition, he comments not only that United States will have a shortage of four million health care workers, but that this problem has been ignored. American physicians and nurses are deployed to work and retrain overseas.

Furthermore, in the year 1999, donations given by philanthropists for health related programs—for instance, in sub-Saharan Africa—amounted to $865 million. From 2001 to 2005, donations dedicated to world health problems increased dramatically. The donations were not just coming from America, he said, but from overseas and were developed by the Organization for Economic Cooperation and Development (OECD) and the United Nations. The *Journal of the American Medical Association* (JAMA) estimates that if current trends of health workers deployed overseas continue through the year 2020, the

United States could face a shortage of up to 800,000 nurses and 200,000 doctors. In contrast, Garrett (2007) and Donald (2002) concluded that the World Health Organization (WHO) and the World Bank are planning to discontinue the effort to support elimination of river blindness in affected countries.

The article of Carbone (2003) states that drug prices were up tenfold and the market had failed poor consumers that needed drugs the most for onchocerciasis, malaria, and HIV/AIDS. Carbone commented on some writers stating that without luring pharmaceutical companies to profit in producing drugs, drugs that cure high-profile diseases would not be in existence today. "Moreover, to encourage investment in pharmaceuticals, the profit must meet the cost of developing not only the drugs that work, but also the ones that do not" (203). However, Mackie, Taylor, et al., state that "ethical issues are a growing concern for companies, in the wake of a series of corporate governance scandals and the accompanying sharp decline in social and investor trust in firms"; bioscience industries responded to these concerns by developing internal ethical programs (2006, 605).

As a result, the introduction of Merck's free-of-charge ivermectin (Mectizan) helps the vector control (carrier of the disease) to stop the transmission of onchocercias vulvulus (parasite). The writers continue to say "the donation of Mectizan (ivermectin) by Merck & Co. Inc. for onchocerciasis control in 1987 as long as needed was a public health landmark." GlaxoSmithKline donated albendazole in 1997 for lymphatic filariasis and both companies extended their donations to poor countries affected by onchocerciasis. They continued, "Both drugs have wider impacts than those specific to filarial parasites and are effective against a range of intestinal parasites;" Invermectin has an important effect on ectoparasites. Furthermore, annual public health awareness is a continuing effort dedicated to these affected countries. The systems-benefit diagram by these authors is very impressive. Linking local and international NGDO between health facilities, communities, and engaging community in health delivery in drug management distribution and delivery could be a great strategy in looking through the lens of the world health crisis (Molyneus and Nantulya, (2005). The Nongovernmental Development Organizations (NGDOs) are partnered with pharmaceutical companies to combat river blindness.

Pharmaceutical leaders' decision to continue support river blindness research is an important one for West Africa and Latin American countries. However, the decision to discontinue the support could have devastating effects on people who relied upon pharmaceutical leaders' promises. That the medicine would be unaffordable to the community and is not worth the effort can be considered as an ethical dilemma for those who are involved.

The program's focus on eliminating blackfly (simulium) breeding on moving waters would not be a good investment because the research is costly and so is the medical treatment. Although the pharmaceutical industry's goal is to help these countries, if there is a zero return of investment, companies are unable to sustain support. However, these ethical dilemmas have not been systematically examined from the standpoint of bioscience companies on how they would address these ethical issues as of yet (Mackie, Taylor, et al. 2006). Furthermore, it has been more or less than twenty years since malaria and HIV/AIDS emerged, and it is still a continuing battle for pharmaceutical leaders. In 1983, Merck & Co., Inc. decided to make ivermectin free of charge for treatment to eliminate blackflies that carry onchocerciasis ovulvus. Simulium blackflies are an addition to already existing global health problem in poor countries. Also, the battle to eliminate malaria, HIV/AIDS, and onchocerciasis continues.

The correlation between social responsibility, performance, and company profit is a complicated one for some. As Davis stated, business ethics as a growing obligation have been recognized and adopted by many business leaders (2000). The company's obligation to the global health programs, environment, and the communities is vital. These communities provide infrastructure for business and its activities. Davis continued, "Ethics in business is not a matter of mere compliance operating within the letter of the law, but should involve a more active posture of doing no harm to human communities and the environment, and doing good wherever possible" (Davis 2000, 270).

We may say the two companies Merck & Co., Inc. and GlaxoSmithKline fulfilled the ethical obligations of what Davis articulated. However, in a time when Merck & Co. and GlaxoSmithKline are planning to discontinue the availability of ivermectin due to lack of funding, would we consider the Merck & Co., Inc. decision an unethical act? Furthermore, investors for drug treatment overseas have their doubts whether to continue to invest in poor countries. Empirical research studies show investing in medical research and treatment is risky business. The article of Orlitzy and Benjamin stated, "True economic performance, however, manifests itself in both high financial return and low financial risk" (2001). The measurement of return on investment positively correlates with corporate social performance.

Program evaluations on projects overseas is a very important step for Merck & Co., Inc., GlasxoSmithKline, and other companies involved. The text of Posavac and

Carey explains the very important aspect of program evaluation process. Fiscal, "objective evaluations require calculations of the financial investment needed to support a program and the return on that investment" (2007, 26).

Another area to examine is the improvement-focused approach for program development. The criterion is an effective evaluation approach because it serves the needs of stakeholders and participants of the program. The case of Merck & Co., Inc. and other companies concerning ethical issues can be very difficult to define. However, in the textbook of Trevino and Nelson, "Moral awareness is considered the first stage in the ethical decision-making process" (2207, 16). Despite monetary loss due to research expense, Merck & Co., Inc. perhaps was aware that the company would be facing ethical dilemmas in the future. After all, the free-of-charge Ivermectin created a precedent for Merck & Co., Inc. to discontinue support, therefore, a moral awareness was first considered. However, according to Green that moral agent is the "highest degree of moral status and possess full and equal fundamental rights, including prima facie rights to life and liberty" (2005, 44).

Overall, for argument's sake, two factors influencing ethical beliefs and decision making are the individual factors and situational factors. First, let us take a closer look at the beliefs of company leaders—such as the CEOs, managers, and administrators—and their values, and moral statuses, but before we proceed, we will not forget: "Corporations are subject to moral evaluation does not imply that corporations are moral persons" (Weiser 1988, 735). According to Trevino and Nelson, "Classical economists assume that practically all human behavior, including altruism, is motivated solely by self-interest-that humans are purely rational economic actors who make choices solely on the basis of cold cost/benefit analyses" (2007, 24). However, the new finding is that people are very moral and rational. When corporate profits and social responsibilities collide, what are leaders' responses to the public, to stakeholders, and to shareholders?

Chapter 3
ETHICAL DILEMMAS

The Pharmaceutical and Biotechnology Industries' Ethical Dilemma

Every case differs slightly, but the rules and regulations should be similar. Depending on the so-called unethical act by the company or organization, the response of leaders, staff, members, and employees responsible for the act will be different. Let us focus on two industries united to tackle world's health crises, the pharmaceutical and the biotechnology research companies. For instance, when the Tylenol recall was launched, according to sources, "Johnson & Johnson top management turned to the credo for guidance. It was important for Johnson & Johnson to be responsible in working for the public interest." On Monday, October 3, 1982, James Burke called for a staff meeting. Personnel in the public, medical, regional, FDA, and Narcotic government departments were notified and alerted of the crisis. The production of Tylenol was stopped, and this was followed by a nationwide recall, during which Johnson & Johnson established toll-free crisis phone lines for consumers and other people who are affected by the crisis (Trevino and Nelson 2007). The text by Gray notes that before the incident, James Burke was prepared for the Tylenol crisis by being knowledgeable of the organizational culture of the company. He acknowledged integrity is a necessary component of employee values. Integrity is the foundation to build a sound reputation and public trust (2008, 116).

Meanwhile, biotech and pharmaceutical companies such as Merck & Co., Inc. encountered the following ethical dilemmas:

- consumers' trust versus broken promises
- corporate profit versus social responsibility
- market vulnerability versus continuing obligations
- social obligations and stakeholders' decisions
- global citizenry versus US crumbling health issues
- legal infrastructure versus bioscience deterring innovation
- drugs that treat illness versus drugs for routine parts of life

Merck & Co., Inc. must decide which way to go for possible responses to these ethical dilemmas. What choices do they have left when things are not in their favor?

Consumers' Trust versus Broken Promises

The death toll of diseases such as AIDS, malaria, and onchocerciasis cannot be ignored. Onchocerciasis is an addition to an ongoing world health crisis. According to Carbone, "The single biggest factor was the development of antiretroviral drugs that were priced between US $10,000 and US $15,000 a year—ten times their manufacturing costs. The poor have no consumer power, so the market has failed them;" he commented to an author about this issue, saying those consumers who cannot pay the drug will die (2003, 203).

Merck & Co., Inc.'s response is to donate drugs to affected countries. In the case of river blindness, the drug called Mectizan or Ivermectin was donated to 9 of the 11 countries affected by river blindness, with 15 million treatments in year 2005 alone. In 2003 to 2007, therapeutic annual distribution covered 85 percent of affected areas (Thylefors and Alleman 2006, 742). Meanwhile, there was a possibility that the drugs production would be discontinued. The possibilities were addressed when Merck & Co., Inc. donated Ivermectin to countries that were affected by the devastating disease. Although, Merck & Co., Inc. suffered financial losses, promises were fulfilled to the public to restore trust in the company.

Corporate Profits versus Social Responsibility

As discussed, the growing ethical concern for many pharmaceutical companies is having to choose between social responsibilities and corporate profits.

The socioeconomic factors in the countries mentioned seem to be the reasons for not producing any more drugs to cure river blindness—or any kind of drug because of the fact that cost-effectiveness is not achieved. The expense of research alone is costly. Furthermore, according to Carbone, the growth of pharmaceutical companies "over the last twenty years has depended on the combination of large, risky investments in research and development with monopoly profits secured through patent protection of the successful products," and these first-time profits in pharmaceutical and biotech companies listed in *Fortune* 500 companies were under assault (2003, 203). The possible responses to these dilemmas are from companies and world leaders joined together; biotech research, pharmaceutical companies, the world's leaders, and the world foundations join together to conquer the world's health crisis (Molyneux and Nantulya 2005). Issues of corporate profit and social responsibility are uniting companies. Is it possible that being united can truly solve the world health crisis?

In an article titled "Toward a Full Theory of Moral Status," the author, Greene, has four central principles:

1. Moral agents
2. Human community
3. Life and sentience
4. Ecological importance

Out of these four central principles, the first one listed, moral agents, contains the highest degree of moral status and possesses full, equal rights and the right to freedom. It is in contrast with human community because human communities lack a moral agency, but they might have similar, full moral status, as moral agency and as human beings. Meanwhile, sentience has quite a low moral status given the ecological importance of the living and the nonliving due to ecosystem relativity. In summary, Carbone continued, these are principles and there are no deeper justifications (44). Carbone says, "Without the lure of profits, the AIDs drugs might not exist. Moreover to encourage investment in pharmaceuticals, the profits must meet the cost of developing not only the drugs that worked, but also the ones that do not" (2003, 203).

Market Vulnerability versus Continuing Obligations

Capital funding is hard to come by in this current environment because it is risky to invest. How then can pharmaceutical companies continue with their social obligations? In the year 2000, stocks of biotech research companies overall were down to 41 percent. During the stock boom, investors purchased stocks that were riskier to seek above market returns. But when stocks are down, venture capitalists are unwilling to take the risk. "Even if nothing about the biotech industry had changed, therefore, raising private funds for research and development is like to become a more difficult task" (Carbone 2003, 206). The possible responses are therefore that biotech research and traditional pharmaceutical companies are partnered together to conquer the world health crisis and continue their obligations to the local and global public.

Social Obligations and Stakeholders Decisions

In the year 2002, the Onchocerciasis Control Programme (OCP) presented the accomplishment of the river blindness disease project. It was announced at a ceremony by Gro Harlem Brundtland, a former World Health Organization director-general in West Africa. These announcements covered the successes of the OCP, explaining that

- there were six hundred thousand blindness cases were prevented;
- there were eighteen million children born in areas freed from risk of blindness; and
- the twenty-five million hectares of land were declared safe for resettlement—equating to the protection of 1.2 million square kilometers, with thirty million people in areas where active transmission of onchocerciasis had been occurring. (Basanez, Pion, et al. 2006, 1454)

However, these obligations and efforts are continuing responsibilities throughout the world.

Furthermore, when stock was booming, investors invested and purchased riskier stocks to seek above-market returns, but when stock was down investors were unwilling to purchase products they knew were risky. The possible responses to this situation are coming from the rich willing to donate money, such as the Bill & Melinda Gates which has given $6.6 billion for global health programs; the United States from which giving tripled after independent sectors and Americans donated $7.4 billion for disaster relief and $22.4 billion for domestic and foreign health programs and research; and the Bush administration which raised donations from $11.4 billion in 2001 to $27.5 billion in 2005 (Garret 2007).

Chapter 4
GLOBAL CITIZENRY VERSUS US CRUMBLING HEALTH ISSUES

Drugs that Treat Illness versus Drugs for Routine Parts of Life

As a volunteer for neglected and abused children in America, I have sought and witnessed the struggles of children and parents to get out of drug addiction. Drug misuse opens the door for these individuals to use over-the-counter (OTC) drugs for recreational purposes, leading many to wonder if the pharmacy's counter and the shelves should be enclosed and all purchases recorded to help find abuse of OTC drugs. In the future, part two of the book "Through the lens of the World Health Crisis" I plan to develop a narrative in mental illness in United States, which is an overwhelming problem that I believe is partly due to society's mentality and habit of every pain pill can solve the pain. Humans lose the ability to let the physical body heal itself; therefore, taking drugs unconsciously is the result. Another serious issue is on how parents are raising their children. This issue is similar to the example given in this book in the introduction section of a five-year-old child diagnosed with ADHD, who was taking seven types of medications, four of which he did not need. The medications affected his mental state and made his condition even worse. The mother of this boy had been abusing drug and alcohol and also had a psychological problem. The boy would hallucinate and had developed a tendency to very violent outbursts. I came in after an event in which the boy hit people and his eyes blinked frequently. The boy developed mental illnesses, plus the disease he'd had from birth from a drug-and-alcohol-addicted mother.

When the rich and the famous indulge with drugs to numb themselves, we shovel this issue under the rug. In a pluralistic society, where celebrities are very influential individuals for our young children, an acceptance of indulgence in drugs is outrageous. We might wonder, *Is it because corporate profit is very much achieved*? Where is the social responsibility that we are all supposed to have within our consciences?

There are overwhelming issues of drug abuse for the poor and the rich. When the rich and famous in the United States indulge in drugs, the middle class, the poor, the hard workers and the healthy suffer. Based on my observation, celebrities affected by this pill mill industry and Hollywood's negative influence in the society somehow are accepted and welcomed. Celebrities are influential figure in the society. However, it seems that our children have become the consumers of a pill mill industry. I am puzzled about this type of new trend of acceptance in society. The citizens of United States of America are over-dependent on drug use for the treatment of minor illnesses in addition to already crumbling local and global health issues. The demand of drug use is overwhelming.

I am not saying that we should neglect those citizens who truly need drugs. I question the ones who do not need, yet they want drugs for their little pain and suffering, those who want a happiness pill that becomes a habit and a routine of life. They seem willing to pay any cost, especially to those who can afford the drugs or rely on insurance companies for co-pays. This surge of drug needs a good profit for a company to be involved. In addition to a good profit for drug companies, medical doctors are blindsided by their patients and ordinary people who insist on having drugs for what they think they need. As a result, this forces doctors to prescribe medications for them. Are health care industries prepared for these forces and the new trend of acceptance?

According to sources, "biotechnology's financial success depends on the public's ability and willingness to buy its products" (Carbone 2003, 207; Mackie, J.E., Andrew D. Taylor, et al. 2006). The possible response to this issue is now under investigation. However, are we investigating the poor, who use their welfare money to buy OTC drugs for recreational purposes to develop their own creativity to be high? And for the poor, neglected, and abused children affected by these types of forces in the health care industry, shall we do nothing? Whether it is wise to buy expensive drugs or alter drugs for generic brands, the investigation by consumers, stakeholders, investors, individuals and other companies is ongoing. Investors must decide whether to invest in drugs that are not life saving. It is to the investors that we must place the question of whether or not drugs are truly needed and if drugs will be expensive or affordable? Carbone continues to write, "Economist like Hammer speculate that drug companies who enjoy patent enforced monopolies in the developed world ought to benefit from a regime that creates additional demand through lower-priced sales to those who would otherwise not buy the drug at all" (209).

A Closer Look at Hollywood Celebrities

How would a pharmaceutical and biotechnology company discontinue producing expensive drugs that are in high demand for rich and famous celebrities? The popularity of these types of drugs must be generating good profits for the company. In this situation, I am puzzled about how companies balance corporate profit and social responsibility. Are pharmaceutical researchers and doctors responsible for these actions by the rich celebrities and ordinary citizens? For example, OTC drugs that are misused and readily available profitable for pharmaceutical industries, but we may wonder if social responsibility has to be implemented for the sake of humanity. In an article by Burns and Boyer, the abuse of pharmaceutical drugs is cited as a major growing health problem in the United States (2003). Others abuse OTC drugs—which are too many to mention here—such as cough and cold medicines for the truly sick. Burns and Boyers (2003) stated, "Abuse of over the counter (OTC) antitussive preparations is a continuing problem in the United States and throughout the world" (75). The abusers are not just ordinary citizens, but popular athletes and celebrities have been found to misuse drugs containing codeine. Our children adore and are influenced by popular celebrities who are drug addicted. The society somehow accepts this type of public influence, including celebrities' behavior as drug addict individuals.

A Closer Look at Our Children and Deteriorating Nuclear Family Structure

In 2006, 3.1 million people aged 12 to 25 had used OTC cough and cold medicine to get high. It has been well documented for a decade that parents and children misuse dextromethorphan (Burns and Boyer 2013). There are serious results of the drug's misuse. The results are dangerous—serious neurotoxicity, cardiotoxicity, hepatotoxicity, and even death. Besides, drug misuse in families can be among the causes of the world health crisis. The economic initiatives and legislative and educational explanations may have to be involved in the implementation of social responsibility. In addition to a deterioration of the nuclear family, an added problem in health care, such as the progression of mental health issues in United States, continues.

Chapter 5

LEGAL INFRASTRUCTURE VERSUS DETERRENTS TO BIOSCIENCE INNOVATION

In the year late 1970s, federal research funds benefitted biotechnology industries. The biotechnology industry was a profitable industry until the beginning of the 1980s. Although, federal research funds was available but did not last, but private research funds tripled motivated by drug discoveries by pharmaceutical industries (Carbone 2003, 205). Since then, more drug discoveries have taken place, benefitting not only the United States, but also the whole world. However, these drugs are very much needed in the poorest countries in the world.

The patent infrastructure dilemma is a possible deterrent to bioscience innovation, which affects the production of life-saving drugs. One possible response to this issue is that, according to Carbone, Jeremy Waldron's Good Samaritan philosophy motivated pharmaceutical companies with his philosophy, the "cost of replicating proven drugs tends to be small, they could provide enough to save some patients who would otherwise die at a small cost . . ." (213-214).

Overall, we should remember Weiser mentioned a corporation is an entity and not a person. However, corporations are responsible for unethical acts created by their employees, and to themselves, "corporations are held accountable because any action done by a corporation is done by humans" (735). On the other hand, the text by Bolman and Terrence titled "Reframing Organization" explains the word "reframing" or "frames" (2003). We may understand what the words mean, seeing the past and the future through mental models of mindsets, schemas, and cognitive lenses focused on the internal and external futures of companies and, perhaps, self-interests. We may question, "Is a world of power, conflict, self-interest, and political games inevitably a jungle in which the only rule is that the strong devour the weak?" (198). The article by Green answers this question. "It begins with the theoretical observation that, since the purpose of morality is to protect rational beings and furnish principled guidance for their conduct, moral agents: are just those rational beings that are able to understand respect moral principles" (45). What if organizations or individuals are caught up between incompatible alternatives?

Proposed policy demonstrates the benefits and results through the analysis of differing ideas, including my writings and understanding of the industry. Selecting the best leaders internally and externally can be based on good research, combining the knowledge of leaders' moral statuses, visions, and mission goals. Today, the number one accountability of organizations includes but is not limited to ethical issues. Companies are determined to seek answers and solutions to solve everyday events of ethicality. For instance, a code of ethics by Gray states that companies develop written codes or credos and distribute them to employees (1998). However, the list of code of ethics alone is not a solution to the problem. Organizations must develop innovations of codes of ethics or credo trainings, and undergo constant reinforcements of credos through talks by management, videos, newsletters, articles, and posters. In addition, an organization's ethical values must be reflected throughout the organization, at every level, and on-the-job behavior must be enforced. An organization's program and goals regarding ethical values are monitored and evaluated regularly (121). The results will be measured through the leaders' values, beliefs, moral statuses, and situational factors. According to Ford, leaders' ethical decision making can be based on two individuals' decisions, behaviors, and environmental influences. The ethical-decision model is divided into two broad categories: the individual factors and the situational factors (Ford, 205). The following are the two broad categories of ethical decision-making models and its elements by Ford (1994).

Individual Factors	Situational Factors
• personal attributes	• referent groups
• education and employment background	• peer group influence
	• top management influence
• type of education	• reward and sanctions
• years of education	• code of conducts
• employment and years of employment	• type of ethical decision
	• organizational factors
• personality, beliefs, and values	• organizational effects
• Machiavellianism	• organizational size
• locus of control	• organizational level
• other variables	• industry factors
	• industry type
	• business competitiveness

(Ford 1994)

What are the contents in the code of ethics that we must implement in our everyday decision making about whether to go to work or stay at home? With today's technology, we can download a code of ethics and principles easily for our organizations. Here are the highlights of places where you can get help.

The Society for Human Resource Management, concerning on how to structure your code of ethics, includes the following:

- memorable title
- leadership letter
- table of contents
- introduction-prologue
- core values
- code of provision-substantive matters
- information and resource

In every organization, each one of us faces ethical challenges. Professionals and individuals are equally responsible for how we govern ourselves—our reputations are at stake—serving the needs of stakeholders, constituents, communities, and our family (http://www.shrm.org/ethics/introduction.asp, 2007).

Chapter 6
IN CONCLUSION

Most of us would say this theory of neoclassical economics that corporations must generate profit to stay afloat somehow forgot to take into account that social responsibility has to be considered as well. When a nuclear family is destroyed due to drug misuse and good ethics are not practiced within the family, children are susceptible to neglect and abuse due to deterioration of family unity. In this country, this issue, which has been neglected for decade, is still continuing at a fast pace. Where should the health care industry and other companies stand when profit is put before social responsibilities? This question is truly confusing.

Should we make sure that social responsibility comes ahead of profit? Perhaps we may say that pharmaceutical companies and doctors are responsible for these overdosed and addicted individuals? Should each individual develop an awareness or be educated enough for his or her own sake and have enough good wisdom to know the difference between bad and good decisions? Shall we apply this philosophical theory to the human community's lack of moral agency, but still grant full moral status, as moral agency, to all human beings? Due to ecosystem relativity, sentience has quite low of moral status is that an ecological importance to the living and nonliving? It means that we as humans unconsciously and unexplainably exercise the activities of morality and immorality. Therefore, for profits sake are these nonmotivated, nonseekers of knowledge are the prey of these companies? To simply illustrate, these drug addicted people are the consumers of these types of companies. Does the principle have a deeper justification? That means, I can ask a question on why companies taken advantage of these type of people to profit?

Are companies determined to seek answers and solutions to solve the everyday events of ethicality? Today, as Gray stated, that code of ethics alone is not the solution (1998). Although companies develop and distribute written codes or credos, how do companies know that employees have accepted the codes and applied them to their work? Constant references to and reinforcement of credos—via trainings, seminars, webinars, articles, and video presentations—may help lower the growing incidents of ethical dilemmas and mishaps. In every level, on-the-job behavior must reflect the organization's ethical values. We must keep in mind the priority of what comes first—the consequences or choosing corporate profit or social responsibility. If we choose corporate profit first, then what are the consequences and the benefits of choosing corporate profit? The questions below will guide you in making a decision for the sake of your company and the society.

- What would you lose and gain in choosing social responsibility?
- Will your company be gaining reputation or profit?
- What is the most important value of your organization?
- Does your organization survive when reputation is lost?
- How does profit survive when an organization has lost its reputation?
- By choosing social responsibility, does your organization lose its profit?
- How does your organization keep afloat when you lose profit?

There are too many questions and no definite answers. Perhaps balance is the key. You may decide to follow your gut. However, please make a decision based on the outcome of the future. Whether or not your company will benefit from your decision or lose its profit, perhaps the end result is good for all—for your company and your company's social responsibilities.

References

Kathryn S. Aultman and Edward D. Walker, Managing Risks of Arthropod Vector Research, 2000, (EbscoHost Industries, Inc., 2008), 2-5.

Basanez, M. G., S. D. Pion, T. S. Churcher, et al. "River Blindness: A Success Story under Threat?" *The Journal of Plos Medicine* 3 (2006): 1454-1459.

Thomas S. Bateman and Scott S. Snell, Ethics Corporate Responsibility:Planning and Strategy, 2005, (The McGraw-Hill Companies, 2003), 157.

Brendel, et al. "The Price of a Gift: An Approach to Receiving Gifts from Patients in Psychiatric Practices." Harvard Review of Psychiatry, 15:43-51 (2007):115, accessed April 7, 2007, DOI: 10,1080/10673220701298399.

Burns M. J., and W. E. Boyer. "Antitussives and Substance Abuse." *The Journal of Substance Abuse and Rehabilitation* 4 (2013): 75-82.

June Carbone, "Ethics, Patents and the Sustainability of the Biotech Business Model." *The Journal of International Review of Law Computers & Technology* 17 (2003): 203-218.

Cooper, T. L. *The Responsible Administrator: An Approach to Ethics for the Administrative Role.* San Francisco: Jossey-Bass, 2006.

Davis, J. F. "Economic Growth vs. the Environment? The Need for New Paradigms in Economic, Business Ethics, and Evangelical Theology." 26 (2000): 265-275.

Drisdelle, R. "Eliminating River Blindness: Merck and Co., Inc. and Ivermectin against Onchocerca Volvulus." (2007), Accessed May 6, 2008, http://human-infection.suite101.com/article.

Ford, R. C., and W. D. Richardson "Ethical Decision Making: A Review of the Empirical Literature." *The Journal of Business Ethics* 13 (1994): 205-221.

Garret, L. "The Challenges of Global Health: System and Sustainability. *The Journal of Global Health* 86 (2007):14-38.

Gray, S. T. *Evaluation with Power: A New Approach to Organizational Effectiveness, Empowerment, and Excellence.* San Francisco: Jossey-Bass, 1998.

Green, R. "Toward a Full Theory of Moral Status." *The American Journal of Bioethics* 5(6) (2005): 33-42.

Grinfeld, M. J. "Mental Health Care Reform: How Will the Lawyers Make a Difference in Patients' Rights?" *Psychiatric Times* 17, no 3 (2000). http://www.psychiatrictimes.com/p000301a.html.

Kottak, C. P., and K. A. Kozaitis. *Diversity in the Workplace.* Boston, Burr Ridge, IL: McGraw Hill Custom Publishing, (2003).

Mackie, J. E., Andrew D. Taylor, et al. "Lessons on Ethical Decision-Making from the Bioscience Industry: Ethical Issues Are a Growing Concern for Companies." *The Journal of Plos Medicine* 3 (2006): 605-610.

Molyneux, D. H., and N. Nantulya. Public-private partnerships in blindness prevention: Reaching beyond the eye. *The Journal of* Cambridge Ophthalmological Symposium 29 (2005):1050-1056.

Orlitzky M., and J. D. Benjamin. "Corporate Social Performance and Firm Risk: A Meta-Analytic Review." *The Journal of Business & Society* 40 (2001) 369.

Posavac, E. J., and R. G. Carey. **Program Evaluation: Methods and Case Studies**. Upper Saddle River, NJ: Pearson Education, Inc., (2007).

Richard-Lenoble, D., et al. "Ivermectin and filariasis." *The Journal of Clinical Pharmacology* 17 (2003): 199-203.

"SHRM Code of Ethical and Professional Standars in Human Resource Management" Society of Human Resource Management, accessed September 4, 2007, http://www.shrm.org/ethc/introduction.asp

Thylefors, B., and M. Alleman. "Towards the Elimination of Onchocerciasis." *The Journal of Annals of Tropical Medicine & Parasitology* 100 (2006): 733-746.

Trevino, L. K., and K. A. Nelson. *Managing Business Ethics: Straight Talk about How to Do It Right.* Hoboken, NJ: John Wiley & Sons, Inc., (2007).

Weiser, D. "Two Concepts of Communication as Criteria for Collective Responsibility." *The Journal of Business Ethics* 7 (1988): 734-744.

About the Author

Sofia Laurden Davis, PhD in human services in the school of public service and leadership, specializing in management of nonprofit agencies and leadership. She is currently a Certified Signing Specialist in mortgage and banking industries. At the time of publication of *Through*

the Lens of the World Health Crisis, her dissertation titled "Nepotistic Ideology in Nonprofit and For-profit in Family-Owned and Operated Organizations" through ProQuest UMI is now ready to be purchased.